MY SECRET SANTA

....

Chase Dormer

Contents

1: The Boss

E lliot's view

I check my email for anything new, but just like the last time that I checked two minutes ago there is nothing. I sigh and spin my chair in boredom. December is the most boring time, all the advertsisemnt that we were working on for Christmas have already been completed, and so this month is just number checking basically.

I stop spinning around my little cubicle and grab one of my books from my stack on my desk to start reading. I never finish any of these books, but why not give it a try.

Just as I am about to flip to the first page, someone sneaks up on me and yell, "Elliot! Have we really resorted to reading again?"

I turn around and smile as my best friend stands before me. "I'm so bored," I reply getting up to hug Ella.

"So am I, which is why I have escaped my cubicle from the other side of the room and have come here to gossip with you," she replies cheerily taking a seat on my desk.

"What amazing news have you come to tell me, today?" I ask in anticipation.

"Well, I hear that Simon, the one three cubicles down is going to be a father," she replies.

"Well that's splendid news for him and his wife," I say happily.

"Um...not really, his wife isn't pregnant," Ella whispers.

"Oh shit," I say shocked.

"Mary, the intern is actually pregnant," Ella adds.

"Oh my god, I feel horrible for his wife," I say.

"Actually that's where things get good. Marty and Sarah saw the intern and Simon's wife kissing goodbye before the intern entered the office."

"What the fuck! This story keeps on getting crazier by the second," I reply astounded.

"I can hear you two whispering instead of working," announces the head Advertisement director, Brooklyn.

"Sorry, Boss, I was just taking a water break," Ella says getting of my desk.

"Right... Well now that I have both of your attention, there is a staff meeting in thirty minutes. Don' be late and don't let me catch you guys fooling around instead of working again," she declares before walking away.

I can't help but watch her walk away, what can I say she has a very fit butt.

Then all of a sudden I get smacked in the face with a stack of post it notes, I glare at Ella.

"You're crushing on Brooklyn," she sings out.

"Not true, that woman is a nightmare. She's all work and no fun," I reply.

"Please, you're always mesmerized by that woman, even if she is a little bitchy sometimes," Ella chuckles.

"I do not have a thing for her," I say through gritted teeth.

"Oh come on, yeah you do. She's pretty. She's exactly your type. Tall Brunette with brown eyes and with some attitude," Ella adds.

"Okay, there's so much more to her that. Yes, she is tall, but her hair is auburn and comes into beautiful beach curls that makes you want to run your hand through her hair. And her eyes are like a light honey brown color that is just so adorable. And she's unbelievably bossy and bitchy, but it's so fucking hot," I blurt out making Ella look at me in amusement.

"You're in deep," she giggles.

"Whatever, whose house are you going to for Christmas?" I ask trying to change the topic.

"Oh right, about that. I'm actually travelling to Colorado with my family this Christmas. My grandparents live there and my mom wants to spend Christmas with them this year," she replies.

"WHAT! WHEN?" I ask.

"I leave in three days; my parents got tickets at the last moment. A family cancelled their tickets and my parents took advantage of the situation to grab those tickets," Ella explains.

"Wait, so that means I will be spending two weeks by myself with you leave," I say sadly.

"I'm sorry, Elliot. This was a last minute thing, I know we always spend our vacation together," she replies.

I put a reassuring hand on her shoulder to stop her, "It's okay, I understand."

"Hey, maybe you can spend time with your family instead of being alone," she suggests.

I look at her in disbelief, "I take that as a no. Is your mom still expecting to see a guy come over and you telling her you quit your job?"

"Yes. She is a pain. No wonder I hardly spent time with her other than at holidays," I reply.

"Cheer up, buddy. She might have changed this time around," Ella suggest, but I really doubt it.

Samuel pops his head around and asks, "Hey, you guys heading to the meeting now?"

"Oh sit, almost forgot. Thanks, Samuel," Ella says grabbing me to stand up.

We hurriedly make our way to the conference room and notice the company boss is here today. I wonder what that could mean.

"Welcome everyone; it's so nice to see you all. You might be wondering why I am here, but it's because I wanted to congratulate all of you on how hard you worked these past few months. I'm so proud of you all. So, this year there will be a Christmas party and Secret Santa!" the boss says enthusiastically.

2: Game Time

"Half of you move to one end of the room and the other half go to the other side," instructed the boss.

"Excuse me, when will the secret Santa take place?" Asked one person.

"On Friday, before your vacation. So, you have four days to find a small gift worth $15," explains the boss.

"What if we leave before Friday?" Ella asks.

"You don't have to be a part of the secret Santa then," the boss answers.

"Yes," Ella says under her breath.

"Lucky," I whisper causing her to chuckle.

"Alright, everyone on the left side of the room write your names on a small piece of paper that my assistant will pass out. Then put the pieces of paper into the hat that my other assistant is carrying," instructs the boss.

After a few minutes everyone is done and the boss focuses on the other side. I'm on this side and we repeat the same actions that the others did.

When done, the boss grabs the hat full of names, "I will come around with the hat, everyone pull a piece of paper out. You will be the secret Santa for this person."

Just as I am about to grab a piece of paper, one of my coworkers, Martin, snatches it away. I grab the one beside it and pull it out. I walk over to Ella and open the wrinkled ball of paper.

I gasp loudly gathering Ella's attention. She grabs the paper from my hand.

"Holy shit, you got...," I quickly stop her from saying the name as I cover her mouth.

She murmurs against my hand and I let go so I can hear what she says.

"Sorry that i almost gave it away. Lucky you though, now is your chance to get on her good side," Ella suggests.

We head back to work and I try to come up with ideas of things to give her, but I can't think of anything. I take out the little piece of paper from my pocket and open it reading Brooklyn's name.

I put the paper on my desk and sneakily take out my phone to text Ella.

Me:What the hell am I supposed to get for Brooklyn?

Ella: How about flowers? ;)

Me: Really, Ella?!?! No!

Ella: Fine, fine... How about you get a Christmas card declaring your crush on her? :D

Me: I hate you.

Ella: Love ya too, buddy!!!

I put my phone away and get back to work, but Brooklyn is in the back of my mine. I still have no idea what i want to get her.

A few yours later my shift ends so i walk out of the company with Ella. We say our goodbyes and part ways to get home.

I pull up to my apartment building and park in the basement parking level and hop out of my car. I take the elevator since i am in no mood to walk up the stairs and get off on the fourth floor.

I walk down the hallway to my apartment and open the door to be greeted by my cat, Mia. I pick her up and cradle her in my arms as i close the door behind me and walk into my living room. I carefully put Mia on the couch and i scoot over to the right to lay down on the couch with her.

"It's been a long day," i tell Mia as she stares at me. She meows and walks over to nuzzle my nose.

Just as i am about to relax and take a nap the phone starts ringing. I sigh and slowly sit up to grab my purse and look for my phone. I find it and check who is calling.

It's my mom. Great.

"Hey, mom," i answer.

"Hello, sweetie. I was just calling to see how you are," my mom replies. My mom never calls to see just how i am, she only calls for big reasons.

"I'm good mom, thank you," i say.

"That's nice, Elliot. So, you're coming to the Christmas party next week, right?" she says.

"Yeah, i am," i reply sourly.

"Good! So, are you going to bring anyone special that we should meet?" my mom asks enthusiastically.

I sigh, "No, mom. I'm not seeing anyone now."

"That's too sad sweetie. You're almost twenty-six years old, if you don't start looking for someone you will end up an old cat lady," she says.

I look over at Mia and she meows loudly, "I know she's mean," i say pretending to understand my cat.

"What was that, sweetie?" asks my mom.

"Oh, nothing. And i know, mom, but i'm just waiting to find the right person."

"Sweetie, waiting for the right person isn't good. You're being too picky. How about you let me set you up with some of my friends's sons?"

"No, mom. I told you, i'm not really interested in guys."

"Oh come on, you just haven't given any guy a chance. You might be surprised that guys are in fact nice," my mom suggests.

"Debatable," i reply.

"Don't worry, i'll set you up with a nice handsome man soon," my mom adds.

"No, don't do that, mom."

"I'll plan the whole date for you," she says not listening to me at all.

I sigh and say, "Look i have to go, but we'll talk soon."

"Okay, sweetie. Bye, i love you!"

"Bye, love you too," i add before hanging up the phone.

I lay back down on the couch and grab a pillow to yell out all my frustrations into.

3: Chocolate!!!

B rooklyn's view

I'm pacing around my office trying to stop the anxiety that is building inside of me as I stare at the pile of paperwork I need review. Sometimes I really hate my job; it can be very stressful, especially since I am a workaholic.

There is just no point of really going home at a normal time; no one is waiting for me to get back. Any attempts at relationships in the past have all crashed and burned. My ex-girlfriends have all left because they say I focus more on my job then on them, and I guess they aren't wrong.

I just have a hard time depending on anyone else or showing affection. I'm not a lighthearted person. I wasn't raised in a warm environment. My parents died when I was young and my brother did a shit job of looking out for me growing up. My brother was hardly ever in my life.

I get it. He was sixteen when my parents died, he didn't want to take care of a nine year old, so he left as soon as he could. It would have been nice if he could have visited more though, but oh well.

Luckily, my grandparents took me in. They were very strict and old, but they gave me a home and I am forever grateful for them for what they did. However they passed away a couple of years ago, so now I'm all alone.

I'm almost twenty eight years old and still alone. Many of my coworkers are married or have children and sometimes it gets to me.

It would be nice to come home to someone who loves you. Someone who wants to do Christmas decorations with you for the holidays. Someone to cuddle with on cold nights.

I sigh and decide I need to go out and take a breather, so I exit my office and walk around the advertisement department and notice everyone is on break as well. Wow, is it time for break already? I almost forgot and kept working.

As I continue walking I notice Elliot and Ella whispering in their cubicle, looking intently at something on the computer. I walk closer to mess with them.

"Enjoying your break?" I ask making them jump in fright. They both turn around to face me and Ella immediately gets up to cover the computer screen.

"Hey, there boss. We sure are enjoying the break," Elliot replies abruptly.

"Uh huh. So, what are you guys whispering about?" I ask up front.

Elliot and Ella look at each other, each trying to figure out what to say, but Ella finally speaks, "I'm just helping out my friend Elliot with finding a present for her person for the Secret Santa thing."

"You know that's only two days away. It's going to get harder to find something that time ticks away," I advise.

"Which is why I am trying the good gift today," replies Elliot.

"Good luck with that," I chuckle, "And make sure when break is over you actually work not look for a gift." I wink at them and head back to my office.

I love messing with those two, I especially like teasing Elliot. I'm not sure why. She's a wonderful employee, very smart and hardworking, but I like to keep her on her toes.

I just like her focused expression. I like walking by her cubicle to see her at work; she looks so badass as she gets everything done with ease. She scrunches her eyebrows when she's thinking and slightly clenches her jaw and bites her lip.

I have to admit, Elliot is hot. She's shorter than me by almost four inches and has dark brown hair. She has adorable dimples and blue eyes that keep you mesmerized. She's beautiful.

She must be dating someone, there is no way she is single. She's probably already engaged too.

It saddens me to think she is already taken.

I walk back to my desk and sit down, staring at the pile of paper. Great, today is going to be awful.

Elliot's view

"Help me find something!" I beg Ella.

"I've been trying to find something. I can't find anything that is remotely perfect enough. You might just have to settle on a gift card, my friend," Ella tells me over the phone while packing.

"Noooooooooooooooooo, that's a lame gift," I reply.

"Then get her chocolates. Chocolate is yummy and romantic. It's perfect for a short deadline," she suggests.

"Ugh, I'm going to look so basic," I sigh.

"You are kind of basic. And you procrastinated so badly, the secret Santa is in two days," Ella teases.

"Jerk," I chuckle.

"Well, I guess I'll go out and look for some chocolate. Have fun on your trip. Safe traveling," I say before hanging up.

Just as I am about to get up to go to the store, I hear knocking on my door.

Hmm. I wonder who that could be.

I walk over to the door and open it slight. "Hey, sis," yells my little brother, Max.

I immediately open the door and grab my brother in a tight embrace. "What are you doing here?" I ask.

"Well, I'm staying with you," he declares grabbing his suitcase and rolling it into my apartment.

"You normally stay with mom though," I say.

"Yeah, but since the party is at our parent's home, that means a lot of relatives are coming and they will be using our old rooms. So, I told mom I'm staying with you," he explains.

"Okay," I say watching him go back outside to get more bags. He comes back with another suitcase and a box.

"What's in the box?" I ask.

"A shit ton of chocolate. I stole some from my roommate; he works at a Rocky Mountain Chocolate Factory. This chocolate is amazing, every once in a while my roommate brings some," my brother says.

"Cool! Can I have some for a Secret Santa gift?" I ask him.

4: Whoops

E lliot's view

I finally finish wrapping Brooklyn's present. I'm really pleased with how it came out. I gave her two boxes of chocolate that I got from my brother, a cute merry Christmas mug with Santa and his reindeer and a fifteen dollar gift card to Starbucks.

I take a quick picture of the wrapped present and send it to Ella.

Ella: Wow, you exceeded my expectations. I really thought you were going to get a shitty last minute gift.

Me: wow, thanks so much for the support.

Ella: You're welcome. Have fun! Flirt with Brooklyn!

Me: That I certainly will not do.

I put my phone in my purse and say goodbye to my brother, but he's still asleep. I guess he's catching up on sleep that he lost doing all nights in college.

I exit my apartment and walk to my car to get to work.

At work, everyone does their job for about four hrs until the boss arrives. He calls everyone to the secret Santa meeting. I excitedly walk into the conference room with my present in one hand.

"Welcome, ladies, gentlemen and people in between or not in between. We shall begin our first annual secret Santa game!!!!!," yells the boss.

"Everyone give your present to the person whose name you pulled out of the hat," adds the boss.

Just before I can walk over to Brooklyn, a guy stops me. "You're Elliot, right?" Michael asks.

"Yes, Michael. We have worked in the same department for the last three years, dude," I say to him.

"Yeah, I knew that. Of course, duh. Anyway, here's your gift," he says handing me a clear plastic bag with a bottle of Vodka.

"Gee, thanks, Michael," I say annoyed.

He walks away and I spot Brooklyn who is about to leave the room.

I jog over to her and follow her out into the hall.

"Brooklyn, for the love of god, wait! I'm not a gym junkie like you," I yell out. She turns around and looks at me in amusement.

"Yes?" She asks towering above me.

"Uhhh....," I'm at a lost for words, she looks so beautiful.

"You okay there?" She asks narrowing her eyebrows in concern.

"Yes! I mean, here. Here's your gift. Sorry it took me a while, Michael was giving me his gift," I explain handing her the present.

She grabs it from my hand and gives me a dashing smile. "Thank you, Elliot."

She glances over at the bag in my hand, "Did Michael really give you liquor. For fucks sake, that man is a mess."

"Eh, it was better than what I expected from him. At least now I can drink," I reply.

Brooklyn chuckles, "One, no drinking on the job and two, take a shot for me."

"Better yet, take a shot with me," I blurt out stupidly.

Brooklyn laughs, "I might take you up on that offer one day."

Then suddenly everyone starts exiting the conference room and moving into the hallway to get back to work.

"Well, it's time to go back to work. Have a great holiday, if I don't see you at the office Christmas party," Brooklyn says walking away.

I head back to my desk to continue working.

---------------------Max's view

I'm casually watching tv and eating some chocolate while I get a call from my roommate.

I put the phone on speaker and answer, "Yo, Dylan. What's dude?"

"Max, you piece of shit. You stole chocolate from my car again!!," yells Dylan.

"Ummmm, maybe," I reply taking another bite of the chocolate bar.

"Damn you, Max. Those chocolates are not edible! They are expired. I was supposed to throw all the boxes in a dumpster!" Dylan explains.

I squint my eyes and stare at the chocolate I'm eating. "But it still taste fine," I reply.

"Oh my god, you're eating it! Spit it out. It's milk chocolate, you can't eat it. It's been sitting in the factory for five years, you idiot!" Dylan continues yelling.

I sniff the chocolate and take another bite, I mean it doesn't taste great, but it's not horrible either.

"Are you listening, Max? Are you still eating the fucking chocolate? Stop it! Throw all the chocolate away!" Dylan advises.

"Fine, fine," I say getting up to throw away all the chocolate.

"You didn't give any away, right? You were the only one to eat the chocolate, right?" Dylam asks.

I stopped dead in my tracks, "SHIT!"

"What do you mean shit!" Dylas asks.

"Dylan I need to call you back later," I say before hanging up.

I quickly call my sister and the moment she answers the phone I yell, "Don't give away the chocolate! It's expired milk chocolate!"

"WHAT!" Elliot yells.

Then my stomach starts growling and I get a sharp pain. I start feeling like I need to hurl. Damn I shouldn't have been eating chocolate all day.

"I need to go throw up, Elliot. Just don't give anyone the chocolate, it's five years old," i say before hanging up and running to the bathroom.

5: Consequence

Brooklyn's view

Just thirty more minutes before I get to go home. Just thirty minutes. Thank god.

I cannot wait to lay in my bed and catch up on sleep for the next two weeks.

I start packing up all my paperwork and notice the wrappers I left on my desk from eating some of the chocolate that Elliot gave me.

That girl is such a sweetheart, she's too adorable. The gift she gave me was so cute.

I love the mug and the chocolate taste good. I grab the wrappers and throw them in the trash.

I put some leftover papers into a folder and put in my desk. I pick up my purse and dig around for my keys.

Then a sudden sharp pain hit me. Ugh. Where the heck did this stomach pain come from?

I double over in pain. I feel like shit right now. Nausea overcomes me and I feel like everything that I ate is going to come up my throat. Oh no.

I head for the door and run out of my office and jog down the hallway. Luckily most people have gone home, but the employees left look stare at me in shock.

I keep running and almost run in Elliot.

"Are you okay?" She asks with concern. I don't answer her question, I push her out of the way and head to the bathroom.

I run in and slam an open stall open and start hurling into the toilet.

As I gag and continuing throwing up, I feel someone walk up behind me and hold my hair back.

"It's going to be okay," a familiar voice says.

"You're going to be okay," the woman repeats. This time I distinguish that it's Elliot.

Og god no! She can't see me like this! But i can't help but throw up more.

Elliot's view

"MAX! DON'T YOU DARE HANG UP!" I yell, but it's no use. His line goes dead.

"Shit. Shit. Shit!" I mubble.

I stand up abruptly and run in the direction of Brooklyn's office. I enter the hallway and almost walk into Brooklyn.

She looks distressed and I ask if she's okay, but she pushes me away and runs. I turn and follow her.

Shit. Shit. Shit.

She runs into the bathroom and I go in after her. She's throwing up in the toilet and I walk closer to her so I can hold her hair back.

I feel so horrible because this is all my fault. I should have never trusted my brother with chocolates. He's not very reliable.

Why didn't I think things through. Ughhh.

After a while Brooklyn finally stops throwing up. I help her up and she flushes the toilet. I walk her over to the sink so she can wash her mouth.

"I'm so sorry you had to see that," Brooklyn whispers out to me. She refuses to look at me and it makes me feel worse.

"Actually it's me who has to apologize to you," I reply looking down at my feet.

"What do you mean?" She asks.

"Well, you see. I caused this...," I begin, but Brooklyn cuts me off as she runs back to the toilet to throw up again.

"This is the last time I ever ask Max for help," I sigh walking to Brooklyn to hold up her hair again.

"I feel like I'm going to die," Brooklyn croaks out.

"How about I take you to see a doctor?" I ask her.

"Please!" She groans out in pain.

I help her back to the sink to clean her mouth and hands and we head out of the bathroom.

"Do you need anything from your office?" I ask her.

"Can you get my purse?" She says.

I let her sit at an empty cubicle and I quickly head over to her office.

Woah. I've never seen the inside of her office. It's an organized cluttered mess. Wierd. I thought her desk would be spotless, but there are five piles of paper on it.

Then I notice the opened box of chocolates. I run over and grab the box of chocolates and dump them in the trash.

"Fucking expired chocolates," I mumble as I look around for her purse. I find it under her desk and walk out of her office.

"Could you lock the office please, then lock the department floor entrance on the way out?" She asks.

"Sure," I reply.

I lock everything and help her into my car.

"Thank you for everything you're doing for me. You're so sweet," Brooklyn says.

"Uh.....sure?" I reply stupidly. I know I should tell her it's my fault, but I'm scared that if I do she will refuse to let me take her to the hospital.

So I keep my mouth shut and drive her to the hospital. She is looking pretty bad now, so I quickly get her out of the car and into the emergency room.

I drag Brooklyn over to the front desk and explain, "my friend ate some bad food and now she is throwing up."

"Oh no! Please don't let her throw up in here," the front desk lady pleads.

"Find me a doctor and I promise I won't let her throw up here," I reply.

The lady quickly looks at her computer and finds someone, she tell us to sit down and wait a few mins for the doctor.

I sit her down in a chair and she looks so nauseous, she's ready to pass out. I let her lean her head on my shoulder and if I didnt feel so guilty I would be jumping from joy at this small contact with her.

"Brooklyn Roberts," a nurse calls out.

"Here she is," I reply helping Brooklyn up and pushing her to the nurse who helps me carry her in.

I've got lots of explaining to do to the doctor.

6: Doctor Visit

Elliot's view

"So, what seems to be the problem?" The doctor asks as he enters the room.

"She is having bad reactions to eating expired food," I reply.

"Wait, how do you know I ate expired food?" Brooklyn asks, barely being able to stand on her own.

"Well you ate the chocolates, I saw the empty box in your office," I reply.

"What does the chocolate have to do with anything?" Asks the doctor helping Brooklyn sit down.

"Well, you see, it's a funny story actually," I say trying to figure out what to say.

The doctor and Brooklyn look at me in confusion and wait for me to explain.

"Well, you know the chocolate I gave you Brooklyn. Well turns out, my brother got it from a friends and he told me it was really good, so I wanted to give some to you as party of the present. However, it turns out the chocolate is expired," I say.

"YOU GAVE ME FUCKING EXPIRED CHOCOLATE!" Brooklyn yells at me.

"I'm sorry," I reply.

"How expired," asks the doctor.

"Five years expired," I squeak out.

"WHAT!" Brooklyn yells.

"I'm so sorry," I repeat.

"I don't even want to know how this happened," the doctor mumbles while he examines Brooklyn.

"WHAT THE FUCK, ELLIOT!" Brooklyn adds.

"Let's all settle down. Now, when did your girlfriend start acting sick?" The doctor asks me.

"Oh um...we aren't..." Brooklyn cuts me off before I can explain.

"What!? We are not girlfriends," Brooklyn declares.

"Oh I'm terribly sorry. It's just that you two argue like a married couple," the doctor explains.

"We are not married. We are not girlfriends. We are both single. She is not gay," Brooklyn groans out.

"Actually I am gay," I interrupt.

"WHAT?" Brooklyn yells.

"What else am I wrong about then? Are you in a relationship now?" She abruptly asks.

"No. You were right about me being single," I reply and Brooklyn gives me a small smile. Even when she is sick she still looks adorable.

"OKAY. How about you go outside, miss, so that I can examine your friend?" The doctor says pushing me out of the room.

"I'm actually her employee," I say.

"WHAT! There's obviously more than that going on between you too," the doctor says.

"Really?! You really think so?" I ask the doctor excitedly.

He squints his eyes at me, "Yes. Now stay here while I help her," he says before leaving me and walking back into the room with Brooklyn.

I sit down in the waiting room with such a stupid grin on my face. Then my phone starts ringing and I answer to Max.

"Elliot, you may need to take me to the hospital," he says.

"I'm already at the hospital, Max," I reply.

"What? Why? What happened? Are you okay, Elliot?"

"I'm okay, but my boss isn't. She ate the chocolates. Why do I keep trusting you, jerk."

"I'm really sorry, Elliot. Also, why the heck didnt you bring me along on the trip to the hospital," Max whines out.

"Don't worry, I'll get medicine for you too, Max."

"Good, I really need it. I ate a lot of chocolate and I can't leave the bathroom now," he explains.

"That's disgusting," I reply.

I glance over and notice the doctor and Brooklyn coming out of the room. The doctor walks over to me with a paper.

"Go to a pharmacy and get this medication for her. It will help her get rid of her upset stomach," the doctor explains.

"Okay cool. Also, my brother ate the expired chocolate too, so can you prescribe him the medicine too?" I ask nicely.

The doctor sighs, "Let m speak with your brother and get his symptoms and insurance," the doctor says.

I pass him the phone and they talk for a while and the doctor prescribes him the medicine as well. Brooklyn and I say goodbye the the doctor and we head out.

Brooklyn refuses to say a word on the way to the pharmacy and on the way to her apartment she gives me instructions.

I help her out of the car and up to her apartment. She gets her key out and opens the door. We enter her apartment and I am in awe.

It's very spacious and modern. It looks amazing! She has a white marble theme going on so everything looks very luxarious and sleek.

Brooklyn walls over to her couch and plops down on it. I walk over to the couch and place the bag with her medication on it.

I turn to leave, but Brooklyn stops me. "Thank you for everything, even though you caused everything."

I turn to face her, "I'm really sorry again. I really tried to impress you with the gift and I stupidly trusted my brother when I shouldn't have."

"Why did you want to impress me?" Brooklyn asks sitting up now.

"Um...I'm not sure. I just thought you deserved something special because you're a hard worker and because you're special," I blurt out.

Brooklyn's facial expression softens and she starts to smile.

"Thank you for everything. And you know what I think I'm going to take you up on that drink you offered earlier today," she says.

"Okay...wait, the doctor said you can't drink while you are on the medication," I explain.

"Ughhhh," she groans out. "Fine, we'll go drinking in a few days," she adds.

"Great, it's a date," I blurt out.

"No wait, that's not what i...," Brooklyn cuts me off.

"Its a date," she says smirking at me.

"Oh, okay then. Sounds good. I'll talk to you in a bit then, I do need to remind you about the medicine and that you need to take it easy," I explain.

"You sure its not because you want to talk to me more?" Brooklyn teases.

I start blushing and Brooklyn starts chuckling. "I'd be lying if I didn't agree with you," I reply.

"Goodbye, Brooklyn," I say exiting her office.

Okay. This day turned from okay to horribly bad and now it ended really good. Wow. What a whirlwind.

Date with an amazing girl in a few days. Fuck, I'm the luckiest girl.

7: Alone

E lliot's view

I head home and walk into my apartment. I glance around and don't see my brother anywhere.

"Max!" I yell and get a faint reply from the bathroom.

I walk into the bathroom and find him lying down on the bathroom floor looking horrible.

"Do you have my medicine?" he asks struggling to sit up.

I hand him the bag with his medication and he replies, "What the fuck took you so long?"

"Excuse me, I was taking the girl I like to the hospital because you helped me poison her with expired chocolate," I retort back angrily.

"Okay, okay, I'm sorry. You didn't need to punish me by taking so long with your girlfriend," Max replies taking the medicine.

"She's not my girlfriend," I say.

Max looks at me stunned, "Well you better make her your girlfriend after everything that happened."

"Steps, Max. Everything takes steps."

"Well at least tell me you passed fucking step one," he replies getting up to wash his mouth.

"As a matter of fact I did pass the first few steps. We have a date," I say happily.

"Nice. When and where?" he asks.

My smile falters, "Oh shit. I don't know. We didn't exactly work out the details."

Max sighs and shakes his head, "You useless lesbian."

"I have a couple of days to think of something, okay. It will be an amazing date!" I tell him.

"You couldn't even think of a present to get her for secret Santa," Max reminds me.

"Hey, whose side are you on?" I challenge.

"Yours, sorry. Let me help you plan, I happen to be quite the lady's man back at university," Max boosts.

"First of all, the chocolate idea didn't exactly work out. And second of all, mom said that the girl you liked rejected you though," I say deflating his ego.

"For the last time I didn't know the chocolate was expired!!! And dammit, that was classified information. Mom wasn't supposed to tell anyone!" he groans.

I laugh and help him onto the couch so he can take a nap. Then I grab my laptop so that I can look up nice places to take Brooklyn on a date to.

Brooklyn's view

When I wake up it's already dark out. I glance over at my phone and notice that it is nine p.m. I have been sleeping for four hours. I check my messages and see that Elliot sent me a message.

Elliot: Hey, Brooklyn. I just wanted to see how you are doing now? Are you feeling better?

Seeing her message gave me butterflies. She is so cute and considerate, even though I did get poisoned by her gift.

Most people wouldn't care about you enough to ask how you are after, so I'm thankful that she did. It's nice having someone think about you. So I send her a text.

Brooklyn: I'm feeling better now. I just woke up from a big nap. Thank you for checking up on me. :)

Then I notice that I have another message on my phone. It's from my brother, Lucas. I immediately open the text and read.

Lucas: Hey lil sis. How are you doing?

Brooklyn: Hey Lucas. I'm doing good, thank you. What are you up to, brother?

Am I coming off as to try? Or am I trying to hard? I don't know what to do. Lucas and I have never been close, so I don't know how to talk to him. It's been three years since I last saw him.

Lucas: I've been travelling all over the place, Brooklyn. It's been amazing. Although I have bad news.

Brooklyn: What's wrong, Lucas? Did something happen? Are you okay?

Lucas: Yes, I'm okay, sister. Don't worry about me. I meant that the bad news is that I won't be able to come home for the holidays. I'm sorry Brooklyn; it's just that an amazing offer has come up to travel to Africa. I can't pass it up.

My heart broke reading the text. I was going to spend another Christmas all alone again. I was really hoping he would come this time, but I guess I was wrong. I shouldn't have gotten my hopes up.

Lucas: You understand, don't you, Brooklyn.

Brooklyn: Yeah I understand, its okay, Lucas.

Lucas: You're the best. Love you, sis.

Brooklyn: Love you too.

I put my phone on the bed side table and try not to let the tears out, but it's no use. I feel like a small child stupidly crying out for her big brother and parents, but there's no one for me. No one is going to hug me and reassure me it will be okay.

I need to reply on myself. I only have me and I need to be strong. Like always.

I wipe away the tears and get up to make myself hot cocoa. It helps me calm down when I am upset.

Today has mostly been a shit day and I just want to get through it and move on to the next day. Hopefully I can get better fast.

----

author note: Enjoy this short chapter. I wanted to emphasize the differences between sibling relationships.

8: Who is Blushing

E lliot's view

I wake up bright and early for no apparent reason. I groan and try to shield my eyes from the rays of sunlight shining through the cracks of my curtains.

I slowly sit up and turn to grab my phone from the nightstand. Its eight in the morning.

I throw my phone on the pillow next to me and raise my hands above my head to stretch.

I push my blanket to the side and get up. I walk into the living room and see my brother still passed out on the couch.

I chuckle and walk into my small kitchen to make coffee. What can I say? I'm addicted to caffeine.

As I turn the coffee maker on I open a cabinet and try to figure out what cereal I want. Am I in a captain crunch mood or apple Jack's mood? Hmmm.

I wonder what Brooklyn would pick? Does she even eat cereal or does she actually make herself a healthy breakfast?

Why am I thinking about Brooklyn now? Isn't it too early to think about her?

She's just so beautiful, it's hard for my mind not to wander to her.

What is she up to now? Is she awake? Is she feeling better? Is she worse? Does she just like me or does she like me like me? It has to. It has to be the latter because she made a date with me, right?

Ugh. I hate all this doubtful thinking. I look over at my phone and grab it. I look through my contacts and find Brooklyn's name.

I hover my finger over call, deciding if I should really call her or not. Fuck it, I'm doing it.

The phone rings for four times before I decide to end the call. Suddenly Brooklyn answers, "Hello."

I blank at the sound of her voice. Her voice sounds pretty deep and husky now. She just woke up and her voice is so sexy. I must have stayed quiet for too long because Brooklyn repeats herself and I finally snap out of it.

"Oh hi, Brooklyn. Its Elliot," I say.

"Hey, Elliot. Why are you up so early?"

"I couldn't sleep. Did I wake you up?" I ask.

"Yeah," she croaks out.

"Oh my god, I'm so sorry. I didn't mean to. I just wanted to see how you are feeling now. That and I just really wanted to talk to you," I blurt out. Oh no. I didnt mean to add that last part. Shit.

Brooklyn chuckles and makes me blush when she says, "You're too cute."

"Oh. Um...thank you."

Brooklyn laughs again, "I can feel you blushing through the phone, Elliot."

"No. Not true," I reply.

"Come on, yes you are," she teases.

I defiant say, " not happening. I'm not blushing. I'm not even phased by your words."

"Yeah right, if you were here in person you would ne beet red," she adds.

"In your dreams, Brooklyn."

"You're right. You were doing more than blushing in my dreams, Elliot."

I freeze in shock at her words. "What's wrong, Elliot. Cat got your tongue? Are you blushing like crazy now."

"No. I am not!"

"I don't believe you for a second, Elliot."

"I'll come over right now to prove I'm not blushing," I challenge.

"Fine. Come," she retorts back.

"Fine, I will" I reply.

"I'm waiting."

"I'm locking my apartment door now," I tell her before I head to the elevator. "See you soo," i add in before i hang up.

The elevator opens to the garage and I grab my keys out of my pocket and walk over to my car. I quickly get in and start the engine to reverse.

I exit the parking structure and head to Brooklyn's apartment complex. Before I enter the garage, I tell the guy at the entrance that I am supposed to meet Brooklyn. He calls her and she allows me in. I park and head up to her floor. I exit the elevator and walk down the hallway to her apartment.

I knock once and am about to knock again but Brooklyn abruptly opens the door with a smirk on her face.

"See. No blushing," I tell her.

Brooklyn smiles at me before walking forward to grab my shirt, pulling me into her apartment and closing the door behind me.

She brutally pushes me towards the wall and walks closer so that there is barely any space between us. I nervously start hearing up and sweating.

"You sure you're not blushing? Because it seems to me like there is a little bit of a pink tint to your cheeks," she says.

"Nope. I think you're seeing things," I reply.

Brooklyn chuckles, "I'm never wrong, sweetie."

"This time you are," I challenge back.

"In your dreams, Elliot."

"Yeah, in my dreams you are repeatedly saying I'm right," I counter.

"Nope. Not going to happen," she repeats while getting closer to me.

"You know, you are incredibly bossy and stubborn," I say staring at her lips now.

"You know you like it," she says leaning closer to me.

-DING--DING--DING-

Brooklyn's phone goes crazy and she sighs before leaning away from me. "What's the alarm for?" I ask.

"I need to take the medication," she replies.

"Okay," I say walking past her and sitting down on her couch.

"I can worry about it later," she says sitting down next to me. "I believe we were in the middle of something," she adds.

"No, Brooklyn. Go take your medication." She looks at me stunned.

"Who's the bossy one now," she says.

"That's not the only role I can verse in," I reply. I can't help but start laughing at her dumbfounded expression she gives me after I made that innuendo.

"Who's blushing now, Brooklyn?" I say smirking at her. Two can play at this game. I refuse to back down and let her win this flirting contest.

"I'm not!" She says getting up and walking away.

"Yeah, right," I reply as she walk to the kitchen to get a cup of water to take her medication with.

"So, how are you feeling?" I ask changing the topic for now.

"Much better than yesterday," she replies, " I don't feel like throwing up anymore."

"That's good," I say. I glance wrong her apartment as she swallows the pills. Her apartment is beautiful, but it's so plain. There's not a single Christmas decoration in sight.

"No Christmas tree?"

"No, I don't really celebrate Christmas," Brooklyn replies.

"You're kidding, right?" I ask, but she isn't.

"Okay then, I know what we are doing today," I add.

"What?" She says looking at me skeptically.

"Christmas decoration shopping," in reply jumping of the couch.

"No. What's the point, Christmas is in four days," she says.

"It doesn't matter how long is left. You are in desperate need of some Christmas spirit," I say pushing her into her room to change.

Brooklyn sighs and complies to go. "You know indent like competing when it comes to being bossy," she says.

"Get used to it, I'm never backing down," I reply smirking at her.

"You're annoying," she teases.

"You're a pain in the ass," I reply.

"Touche," she says laughing.

"Hurry up and change," I say through laughter.

----------Author note: I don't think I can finish the story by Christmas, but I don't want to stop writing it. So, it will finish sometime in January.

9: Christmas Tree

E lliot's view

I push Brooklyn out the door and down the hallway. "How about you do the shopping and I stay home," she suggests.

"No can do Brooklyn. Christmas shopping is part the Christmas spirit. You being in the holiday spirit is the goal," I explain as we enter the elevator.

"I don't think it will put me in a great mood. Watch out to the opposite," she groans.

The elevator doors close and I take advantage of the privacy and close situation with her. I turn around to face her and give her a kiss on the cheek.

"Give it a chance, for me," I beg her.

Brooklyn gets over her initial shock of the random kiss and sighs yes. "There better be more kisses later then," she mumbles under her breath, but I hear her.

"Believe me, plenty of kissing. Everywhere, not just on the cheek," i tease making her blush.

"Aww, look who's blushing now," i add raising my hand to pinch one of her cheeks.

Brooklyn smacks my hand away and argues, "I'm not!"

"Yeah, you were, babe," I reply smirking at her.

Brooklyn narrows her eyebrows and looks at me with fury in her eyes. She takes a step towards me and I take a step back. My back hits the side of the elevator and Brooklyn keeps getting closer until she is more centimeters away.

"Look who's blushing now, babe," she makes sure to emphasize the last word.

"Only blushing because you're in my personal space," I counter.

"Sure about that?" Brooklyns asks while staring at my lips.

The elevator doors open and I maneuver around her to get out. "Christmas shopping remember," I say trying to change the topic.

Brooklyn sighs, "We can't keep dancing around the question of why we are blushing. We both know why."

"I know, but I'm not about to give you the satisfaction by saying it out loud or by giving in first," I reply extending my hand for her to grab.

"I'm not going to give in first, Elliot."

"Good," I reply as she grabs my hand and I lead her to my car. We get in and I reverse out of the parking spot then head out to a store.

After a few mins we finally get to the mall. I park and as I'm about to get out Brooklyn asks, "What are we going to get first?"

"A tree," I say getting out of the car and locking it after Brooklyn gets out. She gives me a dumbfounded expression and comments, "You do know that we have to go to a tree farm to get a tree, right?"

"You reminded me that Christmas is in a few days, so where the hell do you think we will actually find a good enough tree? The only left over trees at any farms will be the worst ones," I answer her.

"Oh, then we're getting a fake tree?" She asks me.

"Bingo," I reply pushing her into the store. I lead her to the Christmas decoration aisle and look through the shelves for a fake tree.

"Found it," Brooklyn replies after a while. I walk over to her and it's the very last one on the shelf.

"Look, it's a miracle. The last one, just for us. It's a sign that for you," I comment.

"Yeah right," she says scoffing. I guess it's going to take a lot to get her in the Christmas spirit.

I get closer to her and wrap my arms around her waist. She stiffens in my embrace in shock. "Can you please try to keep an open mind for me?" I beg her.

"Come on, Elliot. What's the point?" She asks.

I guess its ready for stage two of pleading. I let one hand go of her waist so I can push her hair away from her neck. Once her neck is bare i lean forward to place a few kisses. "Please, have an open mind. Please," I beg again through kisses.

Brooklyn relaxes to my touch now and I can tell she is trying hard not to moan. I got her right where I want her to. I know she would rather say yes instead of moan and show me signs of how I make her feel.

"Fine," she finally says.

"Fine what?" I press.

Brooklyn sighs then mumbles, "Fine, I'll try to be more open to the Christmas spirit."

"Yay," I squeak out before kissing her cheek and pushing her aside so I can put the box ch containing the fake tree into the shopping cart.

"No more using kisses to get me to do what you want. Its incredibly unfair," Brooklyn comments.

"Its only unfair if the kisses make you realize how much I mean to you. Would you like to tell me how you feel?" I tease.

"No, I'm not going to lose this game," she replies.

"Fine, then. You can help me pick out ornaments for the tree now," I say dragging her to the next aisle. She groans behind me and follows without another word.

Torturing her is fun. Also, spending time with her is fun too, but I won't tell her that just yet. I'm not telling her how she makes my heart beat a million miles a minute when we get so close or that she causes butterflies whenever she says my name. Not going to tell her how much I crave her touch and how I desperately want to kiss her and push her against a wall. No, I'm not telling her yet.

And it's got nothing to do with pride. I would tell her in a second of what she makes me feel, and I know she feels the same way, but she's stubborn. She wouldn't admit it because she always needs to be on top, she always wants to be right and in charge. I'm not going to back down just because I like her.

Things are about to be interesting since I don't think she is going to budge anytime soon.

Author note: Elliot or Brooklyn? Or both? Which one are you more into? Or more alike?

10: You Win

Brooklyn's view

We are finally leaving the last store. Elliot's car is completely full of stuff, I stopped paying attention to whatever else she bought after getting matching Christmas themed pajamas.

"Decorating your apartment is going to be so fun!" She squeaks out in joy. I can't help but smile, can she can any more adorable? She just always puts a smile on my face, I love being around her. She is such a light, she makes everything better.

We get back to my apartment and the first thing that Elliot does is try unboxing the Christmas tree. "You know we can do that later. We can take a break from Christmas themed things," I tell her.

"No, i need to put this tree up so we can put the ornaments up, that's the best part," she tells me while assembling the tree.

I walk over to her and kneel down next to her. "Elliot, we don't need to do it now."

"But, Brooklyn, I just want to help you get in the Christmas spirit. I have a feeling that you have a bad connotation of Christmas and I just want to show you that Christmas isn't so bad," she explains. Her declaration warms my heart. I've never had anyone care so much to the point that they are willing to do everything to change a bad memory without even asking why it's bad.

"Oh, Elliot," I reply while embracing her in a hug. "How are you such an amazing person.

"I was born amazing. I came out and the doctors were like, holy crap look at that amazing baby," Elliot says.

We start laughing our asses off. By the time I start to calm down there are already tears rolling down my cheeks. Elliot is still a giggling mess on the floor beside me. After a few more minutes she calms down too and sits up next to me.

She looks at me with such a bright smile that is unbelievably adorable. I just want to grab her and kiss her. But I can't do that. That means losing.

But losing really all that bad?

Every second that I spend looking at her makes me less willing to win. Maybe always winning isn't the right decision. Maybe moments like these are worth losing for.

To hell with it. If losing means getting her then it's worth it.

I grab Elliot's chin and she widens her eyes at the sudden movement. "You win," I whisper before pulling her closer to me so that I can kiss her.

Elliot smiles into the kiss then kisses me back with the same passion. I feel her wrap her arms around my waist. We continue kissing until we can't breathe anymore.

Elliot and I break away to take a breath. "What changed?" She asks.

"I realized winning isn't everything," I reply leaning in to kiss her again and she gladly reciprocates it.

Elliot pushes me back so that I'm laying on the floor and she's on top of me. She breaks away from the kiss to look at me.

"You're so beautiful," she blurts out, making me blush.

Elliot traces my jaw and puts her hand on the side of my neck to lift my head up for another kiss.

"I think I'm starting to like Christmas a little bit more now," I mumble into her lips.

"Good, because you still need to help me decorate your home," Elliot replies.

"More kissing now, decorating later," I beg Elliot as I give her another peck.

Elliot chuckles and gets off of me to stand up. She extends her hand for me to grab. I sigh and grab her hand and she helps me back up to my feet.

She wraps her arms around me tightly and I relax in her embrace. "Can we stay like this for a few more minutes," I beg.

"Wow. Who knew you would get so clingy after one kiss," Elliot teases.

I playfully punch her arm and Elliot giggles. She then pulls me back into a hug.

"I'm just craving this right now. I've never really had someone to hold onto during Christmas. I've always been alone," I explain.

"Well your not going to be alone anymore. I'm here for you," she replies sweetly.

"You know, I'm starting to really thank your brother for the expired chocolate."

Elliot giggles and adds, "Me too. Man, I think I'm really hitting an all time low. Thanking my brother for messing up. Woah"

"Don't tell him I said that, or he will never let me live it down," she says.

"Will do," I reply before leaning in and kissing her.

-ring-ring-ring-

Elliot's phone goes off and she grabs it. She checked the person calling and sighs before accepting the call.

"Hi, mom," Elliot says.

"Yes, mom, I promise I will bring the dessert to Christmas dinner."

"Okay, bye mom," Elliot says before hanging up.

"My mom is practically freaking out over the holiday dinner. A lot of relatives are coming over," she says bending down to grab an ornament.

"That must be nice. I haven't had a family dinner in a long time."

"What do you mean? Do your parents work on the day?" She asks obliviously. I dont blame her, no one expects to hear my tragic story.

"No, actually. My parents died when I was young."

"Oh my god, I'm so sorry. I didnt mean to pry," Elliot says.

"It's okay. You didn't know. I used to stay with my grandparents but they passed away a long time ago. And my brother and I were never really close," I explain.

"So, you are going to spend Christmas all alone?" She asks.

"Yeah. It's fine. I'm used to it," I reply.

"Oh hell no. You're not spending this Christmas alone. How about you come with me to my families dinner?" She suggests.

"I'm not sure, Elliot. I dont want to be a bother."

"You're never a bother to me. I know it's very soon to meet my family, but I dont want you to be alone."

"You're too sweet," I tell her.

"So is that a yes? You'll come with me?" She asks.

"Maybe," I tease.

"Aw come on, Brooklyn. We can make out for a bit more before decorating the tree," she suggests.

"I like that idea," I reply wrapping my arms around her neck and leaning in to kiss her.

Elliot breaks away to ask, "So? What do you say?"

"Okay, okay. I'll go."

"Yay!" Elliot yells before grabbing my cheeks to pull me in for another kiss.

Author note: Next update will be on Thursday, January 17.

11: Complicated

E lliot's view

After a while of Christmas decorating and making out with Brooklyn, I had to go back to my apartment to check up on my brother. I have to make sure he hasn't burned down the whole apartment complex.

After the last kitchen fire, I don't like him being alone in my apartment for this long.

I get out my keys and unlock my door and enter to witness my brother is in the exact same position he was in when I left in the morning. "Have you not left the couch?"

Max looks in my direction and answers, "No! I've gotten up to go to the bathroom."

I sigh and push Max's leg over to give me room to sit down. "Where have you been all day?" he questions me without looking up from his cell phone.

"I was doing some Christmas decorating with Brooklyn," I reply grabbing the control to turn on the TV.

"Why? Don't you know Christmas is like a couple of days away? You are supposed to decorate in November," Max argues.

"No. What about Thanksgiving?"

"No one gives a shit about thanksgiving. It's basically a day to just pig out," Max counters.

"Well...okay, yeah your right. But late Christmas decorating is better than never," I reply.

"I can't believe your boss went with that idea the whole day. She must really like you or something," Max mumbles.

I start smiling because he is right. Brooklyn kissed me today! I'm smiling like crazy just remembering how her lips felt against mine. How her hands wrapping around me felt so comforting and sexy.

"Why the fuck are you smiling like that?" Max questions looking at me suspiciously. "Stop it. Your smile is growing. Its weirding me out." Max grabs one of the pillows and throws it at me and it hits me in the face.

Just before Max is about to throw another pillow at me, realization sets in. He drops the pillow and smirks at me, "You sly dog."

"I have no idea what you are assuming," I reply still smiling, which just gives me away.

"You guys did more than Christmas decorating, didn't you?"

"I'm not answering," I yell back throwing a pillow at him.

"The fucking chocolates worked!" he says beaming with triumph.

"No, you're chocolates were poisonous, you should know," I reply.

"But, the idea worked! You have successfully captured Brooklyn's heart."

"Captured? This isn't a video game, stupid," I reply.

"Okay, but you two are together right?" he asks.

"I mean, yeah. We kind of made it very clear that we both really like each other."

"That's awesome, sis," Max says giving me a hug.

While we are hugging, I stupidly think now might be a good time to tell him about the addition to the Christmas dinner. "Hey, Max. So I might have invited Brooklyn to come over for the Christmas Dinner."

Max goes rigid in my embrace and he pulls away to look at me in shock. "You did what!"

"It won't be a big deal, right?"

"Of course it will! You know how mom will react!" Max says.

"But, I'm bringing a date, so won't she be super happy?"

"Let's think this through, because you obviously didn't do this earlier. You're bringing over a girl as your date, not a guy. Mom won't be happy about that. Second, you're bringing your boss. Mom hates your job; she wanted you to be a fucking nurse. Third, mom is a perfectionist and adding a person in this late will make her pissed off," Max explains.

"So, what you're saying is that mom won't have a mental breakdown over this?" I ask stupidly.

Max looks at me in disbelief and then leans back into the sofa. I lean back too and we both stare up at the ceiling and let silence wash over us.

"I really fucked up, didn't I Max?"

"Yup, big time. Hey at last I won't be the fuck up this time," he teases making me playfully punch his shoulder.

"Hey, it'll be somewhat okay. I'll be there so I promise to cool the ice," he adds, "I'm really glad that you found someone who makes you smile like crazy, sis."

"Thank you, Max," I say before pulling him in for another hug.

No matter how hectic my life gets, at least I can count on my brother being there for me. I wonder how hard this time of year must be for Brooklyn. She has no one, not even her own brother with her now.

My heart aches for her, thinking that she was alone all this time. It's sad, but at least now I'm here. She has me now, and I'm going to make sure she doesn't feel lonely anymore. I'm going to make sure she knows how loved she is. I'll prove it to her every day.

Hold up!

Wait a minute...

Did I just mentally say love?

Holy Shit... Do I really feel that way?

Do I really love her? Woah.

That can't be. Right? Like we just found out we had feelings for each other.

I can't love her already. It's way too soon.

Is it? Can you fall in love with someone so fast?

Am I in love with her? Am I in love with Brooklyn?

Fuck. Things just got even more complicated now.

----

author note: Sorry for the short and late upload.Hope you enjoy.

Heads up. There are not that many chapter left!

Also if you would like to support my photography, please follow me on instagram. My username is leslies_pix

12: Anxiety

- -

B rooklyn's view

Holy shit.

Shit. Shit. Shit.

I'm freaking out! I can't believe I said yes to meeting Elliot's family!

What the fuck did I get myself into?!

What if they dont like me?

What if they hate me?!

Oh god no. I can't let them hate me, I love...

Wait a minutes...

Nope. I wasn't actually going to say it. Right?

I can't possibly be in love with Elliot? It's been like a couple of days of hanging out with her. That's hardly enough time to fall in love with someone.

But, she has been working for the company for a year. So, it's not like we just met. I've seen her around work plenty of times.

How could I miss her. She's absolutely gorgeous. I could never keep my eyes nor mind off of her.

And now we are together and I still can't wrap me head around how this all happened. Everything happened so fast.

It started with a secret Santa game and ended with me being unable to contain my distance any longer. There's just something so special about her. That light in her just draws me in and makes me want to always be there for her to love her with everything I have.

There's that word again!

Love!

I've never really felt this way before. Sure, I've dated others in the past, but I've never felt something as intense as the feelings I have for Elliot.

Is this what love is really like?

Is love supposed to feel all consuming yet warming at the same time. Am I supposed to feel like I can barely breathe without her next to me? Am I supposed to feel on top of the world and so incredibly happy when in love?

I don't have any answers. But for once I dont want yo pish these feelings away. I don't want to push Elliot away.

I want to be with here so badly because I'm in love with her.

I need to make a good impression on her family. I need to be so incredibly well behaved and polite.

I also need to bring something. Perhaps some yummy dessert will be good?

I walk over to the table to grab my keys and head out the door.

Elliot's view

"Stop pacing around, sis. Calm down," Max says.

"You're girl will be here any minutes and everything will be okay, dont worry," Max adds pulling me to sit down on the couch with him.

"I can't calm down Max. Today will be a disaster," I exclaim.

Max chuckles and puts a reassuring arm around me, "You've always been the more dramatic sibling. Hey, nothing bad will happen. You'll have me by your side and Brooklyn will be on your other side."

"Thank you, Max," I reply. Max turns on the tv and we both watch a cartoon while waiting for Brooklyn to arrive.

-knock-knock-

"Whose there?" Max jokes as I get up to open the door to let in Brooklyn.

"Hey, Elliot," she says giving me a quick peck which instantly puts a smile on my face. She smiles beautifully back at me and I let her into my apartment.

"Is this the one and only Max?" Brooklyn asks as my brother gets up and extends his arm to shake her hand.

"Yes I am. Unbearably magnificent aren't I?" He jokes.

Brooklyn chuckles before responding with, "Yes, you have certainly blown away any of my expectations."

"I like her," Max says looking at me.

"Besides the chocolate mishap, I like you too," Brooklyns replies seconds after.

"Now you must deal with two sassy people, sis," Max adds laughing along with Brooklyn.

Okay so maybe it will be fine after all. My brother likes Brooklyn, so hopefully the rest of my family will too.

"Okay, so are we already to go?" Max asks.

Brooklyn and I nod and we follow him to the basement garage where my car is parked. I notice Brooklyn carrying a bag and I ask what is in it.

"I brought some dessert," she replies.

"YUM. What did you get?" Max asks.

"Chocolate cake, but don't worry, made sure to check the expiration date," she teases Max.

"Ugh, it was one time, guys," Max whines.

"We will never let you live it down," I add.

Max rolls his eyes at me and I can't help but laugh. My brother always knows how to lighten up the mood and so does Brooklyn.

We make it to my car and everyone gets in. Max decides to drive because he knows how nervous I am right now. I decide to sit in the back with Brooklyn. I just want to be near her for right now and I think she can feel how anxious I am.

Brooklyn puts her arm around me and pulls me in close, "I didnt get to say it earlier, but you look so beautiful."

I can't help but blush at her comment. I haven't worn a dress in a while, so getting that complement from a girl so wonderful like her makes me feel so happy.

"You looks so beautiful too," I respond.

Brooklyn gives me an adorable smile and leans in to kiss me. I kiss her back and the kiss is so gentle and cute, it warms my heart.

"Hey, go get a room," my brother interrupts, "pay back for all the times you have said it to me."

Brooklyn and start laughing. Maybe it will go just fine today. I'm in a better mood and I'm trying to lower my anxiety levels.

Everything will be okay.

13: Meet my Mom

- -

E lliot's view

We finally get to my parent's home and park in the drive way. Brooklyn and I get out, but before walking to the door, I hesitate a little.

Brooklyn turns to me and reassures me by saying, "It's going to be okay." She grabs my chin to lift my head so that she can give me a quick kiss. Then we walk forward together and meet my brother at the door as he knocks.

Not even a second passes before my mom opens the door with the biggest smile on her face. She immediately grabs my brother and squeezes him in a hug. Max yelps out in surprise and pain, and then my mom grabs me and pulls me into the hug.

My mom stops hugging us and her smile falters as she focuses in on Brooklyn, "Oh hello. I didn't know that my children were bringing company, but the more the merrier I guess."

Brooklyn extends her hand for my mom to shake and says, "Hello, I'm Brooklyn."

"Wonderful to meet you, now all of you come in now. It's cold out," my mom says pushing us into the house.

My dad pops around the corner and he comes over to give Max and me a hug. He notices Brooklyn and says hello, "A friend of Elliot's?"

"No, actually she's my..." I get cut off by the door bell ringing.

"Who else did you invite?" Max asks.

"Just a lovely lad. He's a son of my friend, he is about your age Elliot," my mom replies running to get the door.

"What!" I blurt out. I turn to look at my dad, "Did you know she was going to do this?!"

"No. I don't even know what's happening?" my dad replies putting his hands up in defense.

"Oh shit," adds Max.

"Did your mom just set you up on a date?" asks Brooklyn.

Before I can answer her my mom comes back with a guy. I'll admit he has nice features, he looks somewhat handsome, but I'm gay. I like girls. Most importantly I like Brooklyn.

"This is Kevin," my mom introduces him to us. "Kevin, this is my family. This is my husband, my son max and most importantly my daughter Elliot. Oh and this is Elliot's friend, Brooke."

"Mom! Her name is Brooklyn and she is my girlfriend," I reply steaming with anger.

"That's what I said. She's your friend. We don't need to add her gender, that's silly Elliot," my mom replies.

"NO! I meant that we are together!" I try to explain.

"I know that you two came together, duh," my mom says.

"Oh my god, that's not what I...," I stop because Brooklyn puts a hand on my shoulder. I glance at her and she gives me a look to let this go.

"Now that everyone is here, how about we set the table? Everyone follow me into the kitchen to get things set up. My parents and Kevin leave the room.

"This is not what I expected," Max blurts out.

"No shit," I reply rubbing my eyes and sighing from this mess.

"Okay, so it seems like your mom is unaware of how gay you are," Brooklyn teases.

"No, she knows. You don't understand. My mom has never really been that accepting, she doesn't say anything to me, but she always tries to set me up with guys. It's like she ignores my sexuality," I explain.

"She'll come around, Elliot. Just give her a bit more time," Max suggests.

"Max, it's been eight years since I have come out to her. How much longer does she need to process it?"

"Maybe if she sees how happy you are with Brooklyn she will understand?" Max adds.

"Maybe. She has never really met any of my past girlfriends before."

"Oh wow. So I'm the first you have taken to see your parents?" Brooklyn asks and I nod. "Well shit, the pressure just sunk in. I'm already doing such a marvelous first impression," Brooklyn says as she starts to pace around.

I immediately go to her side and hold her in place and force her to look at me. "Hey, don't worry about first impressions. Who cares what anyone thinks, I want to be with you. You make me happy."

Brooklyn begins to smile and she pulls me in for a kiss. I kiss her back and wrap my hands around her waist and I feel her put her arms around my neck to pull me deeper into the kiss.

"Um, guys...Not to ruin the moment, but we should go into the kitchen, or mom will get upset," Max says before turning the corner.

Brooklyn breaks away from the kiss, but I pull her back in for another one. She smiles into it and slowly pulls away again. "We should listen to your brother."

"I don't want to go into the kitchen, I just want to stay here and keep kissing you," I pout.

"I want to do that more than anything, but we need to go, babe," she whispers.

I sigh and let go of her so that we can go into the kitchen, but Brooklyn suddenly grabs my arm and pulls me in for yet another kiss. "I just had to do it one more time," she replies smiling widely.

"Well, I'm glad you did that. And don't worry, there will be plenty of making out when we get back to your apartment later," I tease. She smirks at me and I intertwine our fingers and pull her behind me as I walk to the kitchen.

Like hell I'll let my mom ruin this for Brooklyn and me. I might love this girl and I'm not going to let her go. No matter what my mom says, I'm not going to break.

14: Standing Up

E lliot's view

My mom forces everyone to sit down at the table in assigned seats. She made me sit next to Kevin. If it weren't for Max sitting across from me and Brooklyn sitting on my other side, I probably would have had a yelling match with my mom.

"Pass the mashed potatoes to dear Kevin please, Elliot, he likes them a lot," my mom says handing me the bowl.

"You should learn how to make mashed potatoes for the future, sweetie," my mom adds abruptly.

Before I can reply with a sarcastic comment, my brother speaks up. "Mom, she doesn't even like vegetables that much, there wouldn't be a point."

"The point was to make it for Kevin, duh," my mom replies.

"Why would I make mashed potatoes in the future for Kevin?" I ask through gritted teeth.

"For when you two have a nice dinner date at home I guess," my mom suggests.

My anger is rising like crazy and I can't help but say, "What makes you think I want to go out with Kevin?"

I turn to Kevin and add, "No offense."

Brooklyn tries to put a hand on my thigh to calm me down, but there's nothing that can reduce my anger right now. I'm furious.

"Why wouldn't you want to date Kevin? He's a very nice and successful man. He's an engineer and I'm good friends with his mother. He can help you get a secretary position at his job, you know," my mom tries to explain.

"Why would I want to work as a secretary. I'm happy where I am working and I earn more than a secretary," I hiss back.

"But a marketing company is no place for a women. Why would you want to work as an advertisement agent? That's not lady like," my mom counters.

"Actually, there are an equal amount of women working alongside men in the company. And also, Elliot is really good at her job. She's one of the best at work," Brooklyn interrupts.

"You're her friend, you're probably just trying to be nice with Elliot," my mom says.

"No, I'm actually the manager at the firm, I see all the reports at the end of the month. Elliot always finishes on time with excellent work ethic. She has a real future in the company if she stays. She's the hardest working person I've ever met. I admire her for that," Brooklyn adds making my anger subside.

Damn, how could I not love this woman. She's amazing. No one has ever stood up to my mom before. No one has ever really defended me against my mom.

"Well I know my daughter best, and she is wasting her life away at that company and staying single. She's almost thirty and if she doesn't find anyone by then, then she never will. So stop putting ridiculous ideas in her head, you childish girl," my mom argues.

I immediately stand up to defend Brooklyn. "That's enough, mom. I've had it with all this talk of my work and love life. Brooklyn is right, I'm doing good and work and I'm happy to be there. I don't ever want to wake up and regret what I do and that's exactly what would happen if I left the firm."

"Also, don't you dare ever talk to my girlfriend like that again," I add making my mom look at me in shock.

"Yeah, you heard right. She's my girlfriend and I absolutely love her. She's everything I could have asked for and more. I'm incredibly lucky if I get to spend the rest of my life with her," I continue.

I glance over at Brooklyn and she has the biggest smile on her face. She reaches over to grab my hand to intertwine our fingers.

"Alrighty, so I'm going to head out. Thank you for the dinner," Kevin says getting up and fast walking to the door.

My mom regains her composure and looks at me in disappointment. "I've only ever wanted to make sure you had the world and this is how you treat me in front of guests. How disrespectful."

"You know what, I've had enough of this as well," my dad says getting up and turning to my mom.

"Just let her live her life. So what if she wants to work at the advertisement and marketing company. So what if she's in love with a girl. At least, our Elliot is happy. That's all that matter," my dad says.

"But what if that's not the right choice? What if she ends up unhappy in the end. It's a mother's job to make sure her children are happy," my mom replies.

"Mom, this whole thing of trying to find me a husband and new job is making me unhappy. Can't you see this?" I ask her.

"I...I need...I need to think about this," my mom stutters and gets up from the table to go to her room.

I try to follow her, but my dad stops me, "Maybe you should give her some time. Maybe she comes around this time," he says.

"Well, this turned out much better than I initially expected," Max says.

"What could have been worse?" I ask him.

"The house could have burned down," Max suggests.

I smile and playfully punch his shoulder.

I turn to Brooklyn to see how she feels about me yelling I love her.

15: Love and Presents

B rooklyn's view

Let's be honest. Christmas dinner was a disaster, but I don't care because I'm on cloud nine right now.

Elliot said that she loves me and would want to spend the rest of her life with me. I know that's a lot to say to someone who you just started dating, but I loved hearing it all.

I love this girl with all my heart. I have never felt this way about someone before. I don't know quite what it is about Elliot, but she makes me so incredibly happy.

She just makes me feel so understood and loved and I can't imagine my life without her in it now.

So, after her parents leave the table, I can't help but want to tease her. Just because I love her doesn't mean I'm going to make things easy for her.

"So, I'm like the girl of your dreams that you can't live without?" I ask her.

Elliot rolls her eyes and I can't help but laugh at her action. "Yes. You're everything to me," she admits making my heart melt.

"You're everything to me too," I reply leaning over to give her a kiss.

"This is too mushy for me, I'm going to my room," Max announces, interrupting our moment.

Elliot balls up a napkin in her hand and throws it at Max. He barely dodges in time before it hits him and he sticks out his tongue at us and we all abrupt into laughter.

Then Max gets serious and says, "Everything is going to be okay, Elliot. Just you wait and see. We all want you to be happy," then he focuses on me and adds, "Make sure you take care of my sister, she can be a bit of a dummy at time."

"So can you! Remember the chocolate!" Elliot retorts back.

Max dramatically gasps before saying, "We agreed never to talk about it again, you monster." We all start laughing again and Max turns to head to his rook, leaving us alone.

Elliot turns to me and begins talking, "I'm sorry about dinner. All I wanted to do was give you a good Christmas memory, but I think I fucked that up."

She looks down at the ground in shame, but I lift her chin up so she looks me in the eyes. "You didn't fuck it up. I can't remember the last time that my Christmas has ever been this good."

"But, it was a disaster..." I cut her off.

"No it wasn't. I mean kind of, but not entirely. I like spending time with you and Max. It's been a long time since I've felt like I have belonged anywhere. And spending time with you just feels right, I'm happiest when I am with you. So, you succeeded in making this a memorable Christmas for me."

Elliot smirks and says, "So I made you hate Christmas less?"

This time I roll my eyes and pull Elliot closer to me, "Maybe."

"Just maybe? Are you sure? If you still hated Christmas, then you wouldn't be smiling this much today," she teases.

"Okay okay. I actually somewhat like Christmas. Only because I got the best present of all."

"What would that be?" she asks with a knowing smirk.

"You, of course," I reply leaning in to kiss her again.

After a bit she pulls away to look and me and says, "I love you Brooklyn."

I smile widely and reply with, "I love you too, Elliot."

We kiss, and then Elliot pulls away again. One of these days I'm just going to tie my hands around her so that I can just keep kissing her.

"Do I get a present?"

I decide it's time to tease her back, so I reply, "Of course, but that present is for when we get back to my apartment. I can't exactly show you my present in front of your family."

Elliot looks at me in shock. Ha. Teasing her is so fun, but to be honest I can't wait until we get back to my apartment. Kissing is fun, but there are others things I want to try with her.

Elliot regains her composure and says, "I can't wait to see your present. However, I need to talk to my parents before we can leave."

"No worries. I understand, Elliot. Go on," I tell her.

Elliot hesitantly gets up and walks over to the stairs. She grabs a hold of the railing to go up, but she freezes.

"I don't know if I can face her right now, especially after that dinner fiasco," she says.

I get up and walk over to stand behind her. I wrap my arms around her reassuringly and say, "It's okay, Elliot. You can do it. You're strong. And I know that you're mother loves you. Everything will be okay, just like what Max said."

"But how do you know for sure? What if she refuses to accept me again? What if she disowns me?"

"Elliot, your mom loves you too much to disown you. She really just wants you to be happy, she will come around, and I know it. Most moms are a bit of a control freak, but that's them just showing that they care."

"If my mom was still alive, I'm pretty sure she would be very similar to your mom. They would get along great," I jokingly add.

Elliot smiles at me and looks up the stairs, "Okay. I'm going to talk to her."

"That's the spirit, babe," I reply kissing her cheek before pushing her up the stairs.

I watch her walk up and grab the door handle to a room and slowly open it. She enters the room and slowly closes the door behind her.

I really hope everything works out.

16: The End

E lliot's view

    Once inside my parent's room I find my mom sitting on the bed. As I walk forward she looks up at me and I can see her tear stained face. It pains me to see her like this, she is normally so upbeat.

I sit down on the bed next to her and we let the silence overwhelm us as we both try to think of something to say to each other.

My mom finally breaks the silence, "I never meant to make you feel like you weren't enough as is. I'm so sorry for doing this to you," she says breaking down.

I immediately wrap my arms around and pull her into me so she is crying into my shoulder. "I'm so sorry," she repeats over and over again.

I thought I could be strong. I thought I was going to be so defiant right now. I thought I was going to have to go in fighting.

I never for a second expected this. I never expected an apology.

Before I know it tears start rolling down my cheeks. I have never felt more understand by her.

Finally my mom starts to calm down and she pulls away to look at me. She extends her hand to wipe away my tears. "I'm so sorry I made you cry, Elliot."

"It's okay mom, I know you just always wanted the best for me," I reply.

"No, what I did was wrong. I was so selfish; I wanted to mold you into something you were not. I shouldn't have put so much pressure on you. I should have listened to you all those times. I should have payed attention to the fact that I was making you unhappy."

"It's okay, mom. I'm just happy you understand now," I reply hugging her.

"Oh honey, I more than understand you now. I support you in whatever you do. You want to continue working at your job, does it? Be the best. You want to continue dating girls, do it. I promise I won't set you up with another guy."

We both start laughing at that last part and I add, "Thank you mom. And I don't want to continue dating girls, I just want to be with one girl."

My mom smiles and says, "Your girl, Brooklyn, is a feisty one. I like her. I can see how much she loves you by the fact that she stood up for you so quickly."

"Yeah, I love her too," I say smiling happily.

"Aw, my daughter is a love struck puppy," my mom teases.

"Maybe," I joke back.

"I'm so happy for you, Elliot. Love is a beautiful thing."

"Thank you, mom. I love you," I say hugging her again.

"I love you too, sweetie. Now, get going before it gets too late, have a good afternoon Elliot," my mom replies.

"Bye mom," I say before leaving her room and heading downstairs. Brooklyn sees me and gets up from the couch and opens her arms for me and I embrace her.

"How did it go?" she asks.

"It went a lot better than I expected," I reply.

"See, everything turned out okay in the end. You should believe me for often, since I'm always right."

I roll my eyes at her and lean in to kiss her. God, this girl makes me so happy.

We break away from the kiss and I ask, "Ready to go?"

"Yeah, let's just go find Max," Brooklyn replies and we head over to his room.

"Hey Max, ready to go?" I ask.

"Max is on his computer playing games and he turns around to yell, "Nah, I'm going to stay. Go have some quality time you two love birds."

"Okay, you don't need to tell me twice," I reply laughing along with Max who damn well knows what is happening when Brooklyn and I get back to the apartment.

Brooklyn and I head back to my car hand in hand, as happy as we can be.

Brooklyn's view(2 years later)

I can't believe this is going to be my third Christmas with Elliot and her family. A lot has changed since the first dinner I have ever gone to with her and her family. Her parent are much more supportive and loving and have become like my second parents.

I can't begin to explain how happy Elliot and her family have made me feel. I used to feel so alone and broken, but that all changed when I fell for Elliot. She changed my life. She made every day worth living and I can't imagine my life without her.

This is why I have a ring hidden in my coat pocket for her. I just need to wait about another hour to propose to her, but the anticipation is absolutely killing me.

I keep glancing over at Max, who looks just as excited as I am. I told him what I was planning a few months ago and he loved the idea and has helped my plan everything out. He really is an awesome brother and I can't wait until he becomes my family. Elliot's parents also know as well, I asked for their blessing and they gave it to me.

The only one not in the loop is Elliot, and she is going to be so shocked and happy. I can't wait to see her expression; it's going to be priceless.

I glance over at Elliot and she smiles at me warmly. God, I will never get over her adorable smile, I just love it so much. I love everything about this girl and I can't wait to call her my wife.

It's about time I propose, Elliot and I have already been planning out the rest of our lives together.

I'm going to love this girl to the end of time.

CPSIA information can be obtained
at www.ICGtesting.com
Printed in the USA
LVHW050812301222
736050LV00009B/942